# Super Scientists

## *40 inspiring icons*

Anne Blanchard & Tino

**WIDE EYED EDITIONS**

# Wonder, question, discover

The history of science is full of questions, dramas, scandals and doubts. Whether it is from gazing at the vast sky or peering through a microscope at the infinitely small, trying to solve the puzzles of the universe is an activity as old as time.

Today, students are still taught Thales's theories and Pythagorean multiplication tables. It was by using these discoveries that the ancient Greeks constructed the foundations of mathematical reasoning and rationality.

Although it would be centuries before scientific thought was completely separate from religion, mysticism, and magic, eventually science was divided into physics, chemistry, and biology. The "experimental method" was also established, which meant that in order for something to be proven, it needed to be repeated and achieve the same result each time.

The world's great scientists owe a lot to the early thinkers and scientific revolutionaries: Galileo, Lavoisier, Darwin, and Einstein in particular because their great laws radically changed how humanity understands life, the Earth, and the universe. And let's not forget the women, who, until the 20th century, were largely stopped from entering laboratories and observatories.

There is always more to be discovered, and today scientists are making huge developments in robotics, genetic engineering, and computing.

# *Contents*

**21**

JAMES CLERK
MAXWELL

•

**22**

CHARLES DARWIN

•

**23**

GREGOR MENDEL

•

**24**

LOUIS PASTEUR

•

**25**

DMITRI IVANOVICH
MENDELEEV

**26**

ADA LOVELACE

•

**27**

DAVID HILBERT

•

**28**

MARIE CURIE

•

**29**

ERNEST
RUTHERFORD

•

**30**

ALBERT EINSTEIN

**31**

NIELS BOHR

•

**32**

ALFRED WEGENER

•

**33**

ALAN TURING

•

**34**

ROSALIND FRANKLIN

•

**35**

HGP AND THE
HUMAN GENOME

**36**

VERA RUBIN

•

**37**

FRANÇOISE
BARRÉ-SINOUSSI

•

**38**

TIM BERNERS-LEE

•

**39**

STEPHEN HAWKING

•

**40**

NEIL DEGRASSE
TYSON

# Thales

**Before Thales, people used to explain the world by telling stories based on the Olympian gods or mythology.** Thales decided that this wasn't scientific enough. He discovered geometry, the essential theory of the triangle, and astronomy. Using his discoveries, Thales predicted a solar eclipse: a prophecy that came true and was watched by battling soldiers, who, in their terror at the disappearing sun, decided to stop fighting. He had proven that his method of logical reasoning worked.

## ALL IS WATER

Thales thought that all living things came from water. Although his idea was wrong, the steps he took to reach his conclusion demonstrated logical reasoning. This marked the beginning of science as we know it.

### CONTEXT

Before Thales, the scholars of Babylon, Egypt, and Greece had believed that things happened because of the will of the gods or other supernatural beings.

## THE MOON AND THE SUN

Thales correctly thought that the moon did not have its own light source but was actually illuminated by the sun. He may have also understood that the moon rotates around the Earth...

### AMAZING

According to the philosopher Socrates, one day, while deep in thought and gazing at the sky, Thales fell down a well.

## BIOGRAPHY

**BORN**
circa 600 B.C., in Miletus (Greece)

**DIED**
in Tenedos (today's Turkey)

**FIELD**
philosopher, astronomer, geometrist, physicist

**CAREER**
founder of the Milesian School

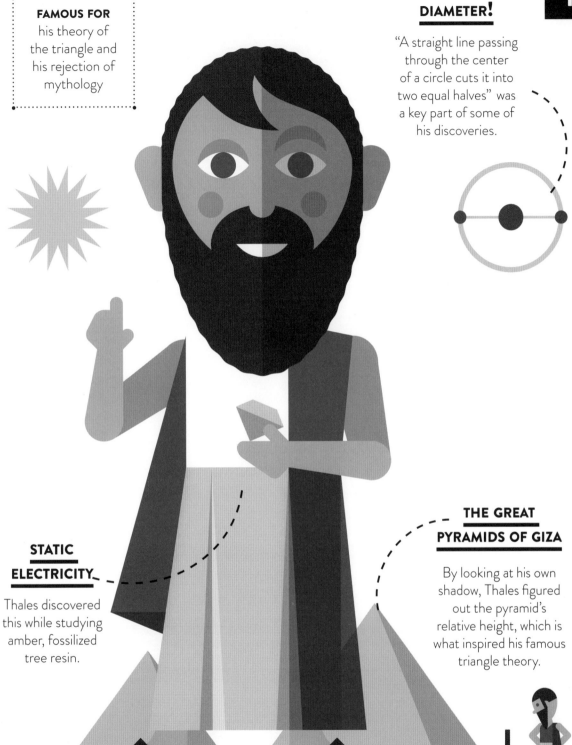

**FAMOUS FOR**
his theory of
the triangle and
his rejection of
mythology

**DIAMETER!**
"A straight line passing
through the center
of a circle cuts it into
two equal halves" was
a key part of some of
his discoveries.

**STATIC
ELECTRICITY**
Thales discovered
this while studying
amber, fossilized
tree resin.

**THE GREAT
PYRAMIDS OF GIZA**
By looking at his own
shadow, Thales figured
out the pyramid's
relative height, which is
what inspired his famous
triangle theory.

# The first scientist

# Pythagoras

It was while listening to music that Pythagoras's big idea struck: numbers were the key to the universe, everything could be turned into numers. The popularity of his teachings created a fan club of loyal "Pythagoreans" united by their love of numbers. Pythagoras was also one of the first to suggest that math, like science, should be based on evidence. He was the author of the famous equation that showed how in a right-angled triangle $a^2 + b^2 = c^2$. You can also blame Pythagoras for inventing times tables!

## 367

is the number of different demonstrations of the equation $a^2 + b^2 = c^2$.

### APPLICATIONS

Pythagoras's mathematical equations help to calculate longitude, latitude, and the position of stars, so they are useful for astronomers and geographers.

### DO RE MI FA SO LA TI DO

Pythagoras discovered that music is math! A note has a higher or lower sound depending on its wavelength. His followers used Pythagorean methods to figure out how different musical keys related to each other.

### KEEP A SECRET

The Pythagoreans kept their discoveries secret by writing them in code. Pythagorean teachers would only describe the methods out loud and there were certainly no class handouts!

### BIOGRAPHY

**BORN**
580 B.C., in Samos (Greece)

**DIED**
500 B.C., in Metapontum (today's Italy)

**FIELD**
mathematics and philosophy

**CAREER**
student at Thales's school

**FAMOUS FOR**
his triangle
theorum

**THE SONG OF THE SKY**

Pythagoras tried to see if the
position of the stars in the sky
had any relation to musical
notes in a scale.

**A SACRIFICE OF**
**100 COWS**

As a way of thanking the
gods for his successful
theory, Pythagoras made
this sacrifice called a
"hecatomb."

**SET SQUARE**

Pythagoras's theorem
helps architects to
calculate right angles.

# The angle king

# Aristotle

**BIOGRAPHY**

**BORN**
384 B.C., in Stagira
(Macedonia)

**DIED**
322 B.C., in Chalcis
(Greece)

**FAMILY**
father was a royal
doctor

**FIELD**
philosophy

**In the newly built city of Athens, Aristotle was a student at the Academy, where he was Plato's star pupil.** Plato was called "the father of Western philosophy" because he defined knowledge, love, and politics. Following in these famous footsteps was difficult, but Aristotle also became one of the most significant philosophers of the West. He wrote about science, philosophy, and the animal world. He taught Alexander the Great, who spread Aristotle's way of thinking as he conquered large parts of the world.

## DISTINGUISHING

Aristotle thought it was important to distinguish between things. For example, the sky and the Earth, things with souls and inanimate objects, and experience and knowledge of something.

> "We do not know a truth without knowing its cause."

## NORTHERNER

Because he wasn't from Athens, Aristotle wasn't allowed to take over from Plato as the director of the Academy. Instead, he opened his own college, but when his friend Alexander the Great died, Aristotle fled Athens because outsiders were punished.

**INFLUENCES**
Christians and Muslims believe Aristotle's idea that the Earth was a motionless center of the universe—a theory that was believed until the 16th century.

## EARTH, AIR, WATER, FIRE

According to Aristotle, everything is formed of these four elements.

## ALEXANDER THE GREAT

Aristotle's old student Alexander the Great would send him animals and plants from his travels.

## THE SPHERES

Aristotle considered that the universe was made up of concentric spheres all encircling the Earth.

# The philosopher

# Euclid

**We don't know much about Euclid,** but this mathematician's book *Elements* played a very important role in the foundation of what we call geometry. He was writing in the 4th century B.C., but it wasn't until the 19th century that mathematicians would try something other than Euclidean geometry. Using five "postulates," Euclid defined all geometry in two-dimensional space. The importance of his thinking has left its trace on how we think about the world.

## POSTULATES

A postulate is something that we take to be true without needing to see the proof. The idea of a postulate is essential to Euclidean geometry.

"All right angles are equal to each other."
(Euclid's 3rd postulate)

## THE FIRST UNIVERSITY

Although the Alexandrian School was founded in Egypt in around 305 B.C., it was dominated by the Greeks. It had classrooms, laboratories, and a library, which were well known in the Mediterranean. Euclid taught math here.

**CONTEXT**

Geometry as founded on experience was born 4,000 years ago in both Mesopotamia and Egypt. With the Greeks came a new abstract approach to it based on figuring things out.

## BIOGRAPHY

**BORN**
circa 300 B.C., in Greece

**FIELD**
mathematics, geometry, physics, philosophy

**CAREER**
one of the founders of the Alexandrian School

## THE GOLDEN RATIO

This is a term Euclid invented to describe the ratio 1 to 1.61, which occurs often in nature. It is also used by artists and architects to make things look well proportioned.

1,618...

## ELEMENTS

Until the 20th century, Euclid's book was the second most printed book in the world after the Bible.

## POINT-LINE-PLANE POSTULATE

Euclid's first postulate, states there can be only one straight line passing between two distinct points.

## FAMOUS FOR
his five fundamental postulates of geometry

*The pro postulator*

# Archimedes

**Legend has it that Archimedes** jumped from his bath exclaiming "Eureka!" meaning "I've found it!" Archimedes had just discovered that it was possible to measure the size of an object by putting it in water and measuring how much water spilled out. This is called displacement theory. Because of his ability to combine theory with practice (and bathing with mathematics), Archimedes is known as one of the first engineers, as well as a magician.

"Give me a place to stand and I will move the earth."
Archimedes

## APPLICATIONS

Archimedes figured out how boats are able to stay afloat using his displacement theory. If a boat weighs less than the amount of water it is displacing, then it will float.

## AMAZING

Archimedes invented a crane that could sink boats in war, but it was during one of these battles that he was killed by an enemy soldier.

## POWERS

Archimedes came up with a system of "powers" in order to be able to write very large numbers. As an example calculation, he demonstrated that the number of grains of sand on all the universe's beaches totalled $10^{63}$!

## BIOGRAPHY

**BORN**
287 B.C., in Syracuse (Italy)

**DIED**
212 B.C., in Syracuse (Italy)

**FAMILY**
father was a famous astronomer

**FIELD**
mathematics, physics, engineer

**ENGINEER**

Nuts, bolts, and screws were also invented by Archimedes.

**5**

**THE LAW OF THE LEVER**

"Give me a lever and a place to stand and I will move the Earth."

**FAMOUS FOR** the concepts of thrust, displacement, and "pi"

**1 cm**

**π   (3.1415...)**

Archimedes calculated that "pi" is the relationship between the circumference (outside edge) of a circle and its diameter (the line through the middle).

# The first engineer

# Zhang Heng

**Zhang Heng was the chief astronomer for the imperial court of the Han dynasty.** He invented a detection device that could measure tremors in the Earth and so laid the foundations for the study of earthquakes. He also led the great observatory in Luoyang, where he observed meteorological variations such as cloud formation and wind speed, which was staggeringly ahead of its time. A writer and mathematician, Zhang also attempted to explain the origins of the Earth and the sky.

**BIOGRAPHY**

**BORN**
78 A.D., in Nanyang (China)

**DIED**
139 A.D., in Luoyang (China)

**FAMILY**
father was a governor

**FIELD**
astronomy, mathematics, poetry

## CONTEXT

China has frequent earthquakes, so it needs to be prepared. Emperors encouraged the country's scientists to find solutions.

## SEISMOSCOPE

Zhang invented an urn with a pendulum in its center that swung when there were slight vibrations—which usually happened just before an earthquake. The swinging pendulum would disturb one of nine marbles. Zhang could figure out where the earthquake would be by looking at which marble fell.

## CELESTIAL WARNINGS

The emperor was thought to be halfway between the gods and the people. Natural disasters were therefore thought to be the result of the emperor punishing his people, but Zhang proved this was not true.

## MOONLIGHT

Zhang was the first person to realize that the moon doesn't make its own light, but reflects it from the sun.

**FAMOUS FOR**
his seismoscope and drawing the first Chinese celestial catalog, mapping the stars and planets

**ARMILLARY SPHERE**

2,500 stars have been discovered thanks to Zhang's invention.

**THE SHAPE OF THE EARTH**

Zhang said that the Earth was not flat, but that if the sky was an egg, then the Earth was the yoke at its center.

**9 DRAGONS**

Each hold a marble in their teeth. If the Earth vibrates, then one marble will fall into a frog's mouth.

*A mover and a shaker*

# Hypatia of Alexandria

**AMAZING**

She probably saw one of science's great tragedies, the fire at the library of Alexandria. We know that she taught there and that her students loved her.

**CONTEXT**

As Egypt became Roman territory, people started to become Christian. Hypatia remained Pagan and devoted to the ideas of Plato and Aristotle.

**The first woman mathematician and academic in history,** Hypatia was also known as a famous martyr who died for her beliefs. Before her death, she wrote commentaries and posed famously difficult mathematical problems. Following her assassination, many great thinkers left Alexandria, effectively marking the end of a long century of Greek progress and scholarship. From here, it would be Indian and Arab scholars who would take up the mantle and lead the world's scientific race.

**BIOGRAPHY**

**BORN**
370 A.D. in Alexandria (Egypt)

**DIED**
415 A.D., in Alexandria (Egypt)

**FAMILY**
father was a mathematician

**FIELD**
mathematics and philosophy

## A TORTURED GENIUS

It is thought that the bishop of Alexandria ordered the death of Hypatia. He was worried that she had too much influence over the city's governor. A gang of monks murdered her by cutting her with oyster shells.

## RECORDS

Although Hypatia's writings disappeared, we know a lot about her. As well as her mathematical texts, she edited Euclid and reviewed Ptolemy. Over the centuries, historians, poets, and feminists have made her their icon.

## ASSASSINATION

Hypatia's murder is a famous example of the distrust of smart women in ancient times.

## ELOQUENCE

According to her contemporary Paladas, Hypatia was renowned for being a brilliant speaker.

## PEDAGOGY

The story goes that Hypatia traveled the city explaining the ideas of Plato, Aristotle, and the great philosophers.

## FAMOUS FOR

teaching at the prestigious university of Alexandria

# The first woman of science

# Brahmagupta

**Thanks to Brahmagupta, zero stops being a symbol digit and becomes a number.** Pushing at the limits of abstract thinking, he also imagined negative numbers. In order to share this idea, Brahmagupta explained in his writing that positive numbers are "good" like profit, whereas negative numbers are like a loss or a debt: "A debt minus zero is a debt. Zero minus zero is a zero. A fortune minus zero is a fortune."

## TO EUROPE

In the 8th century, a scholar collected all of Brahmagupta's books and transported them to Baghdad. There, the mathematician al-Khwarizmi, taken with the number zero, dedicated a book to Brahmagupta's ideas, which was translated into Latin and read across Europe.

## 0

Since 3000 B.C., Mesopotamians used "0" as a symbol meaning "nothing," without using it in equations.

## BIOGRAPHY

**BORN**
circa 598 A.D., in Bhinmal (India)

**DIED**
circa 665 A.D., in Bhinmal (India)

**FAMILY**
father was an astronomer

**FIELD**
mathematics, astronomy, poetry

## APPLICATIONS

Zero was slowly adopted by the West during the Middle Ages. Zero made it easier and easier to do calculations with very large numbers.

## A REVOLUTION

It is impossible to measure temperature or altitude above sea level, or use negative numbers without zero. But it took a long time to understand the concept, which did not exist in the Roman system.

### THE EARTH GOES AROUND THE SUN

Brahmagupta calculated that it takes 365 days, 6 hours, and 36 seconds for the Earth to travel around the sun. In other words, a year!

**FAMOUS FOR** defining zero and negative numbers

### JANTAR MANTAR

Brahmagupta was the director of this astronomical park in Jaipur in India, admired by the Greeks.

### *BRAHMASPHUTA-SIDDHANTA*

In this book, Brahmagupta defined zero and how to use it.

# The believer in nothing

# Avicenna

> "I would rather have a short life with width than a narrow one with length." Avicenna

**Ibn Sina, known as "Avicenna" in the West,** famously wrote of his outlandish adventures and even praised his own genius. Made a celebrity through his groundbreaking medical work, Avicenna became a political advisor. However, times were troubled and Avicenna had to escape civil unrest. Eventually captured and imprisoned, Avicenna had just enough time to write an important encyclopedia, *The Canon of Medicine*. When he later fell ill, he knew he would die and he prepared by studing philosophy.

### THE CANON OF MEDICINE

In this book, Avicenna laid out all his clinical observations combined with all the medical knowledge amassed at the time. Thanks to him, Europe would rediscover its Greek heritage, now enriched with Arab-Muslim knowledge.

### CONTEXT

During the Middle Ages, Europe lost many texts written by the ancient Greeks. Fortunately, Arab scientists are slowly recovering them.

### A PRODIGY

At the age of 18, Avicenna decided his medical training was complete. Describing 800 medicines and remedies would take a little longer than his education, but many of them we still use today in both the East and West.

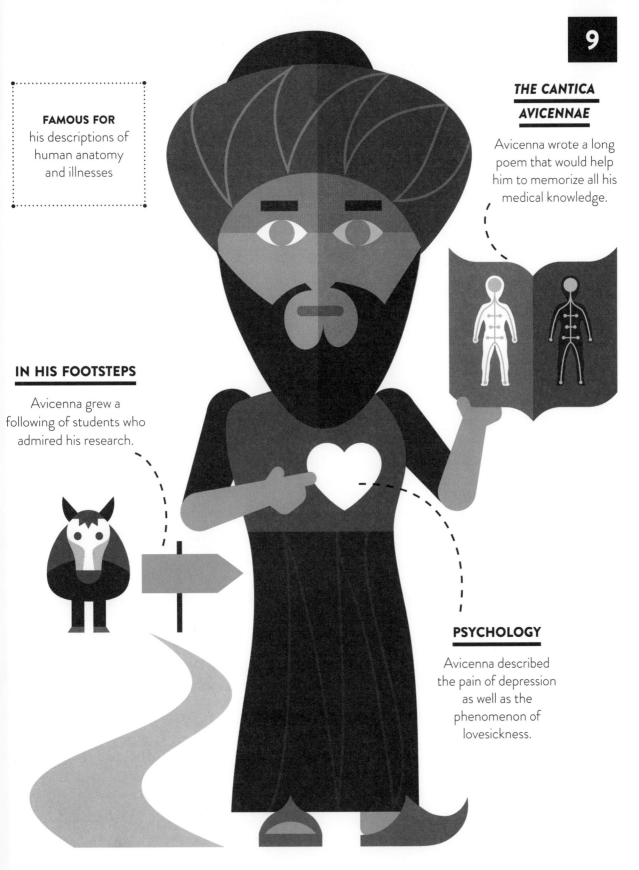

**FAMOUS FOR**
his descriptions of human anatomy and illnesses

**THE CANTICA AVICENNAE**
Avicenna wrote a long poem that would help him to memorize all his medical knowledge.

**IN HIS FOOTSTEPS**
Avicenna grew a following of students who admired his research.

**PSYCHOLOGY**
Avicenna described the pain of depression as well as the phenomenon of lovesickness.

# The good doctor

# Alhazen

**The Iraqi Ibn al-Haytham, known as Alhazen in the West,** studied the nature of light, the workings of the eye, and the mechanisms of vision. His *Book of Optics* is as precise and detailed as a modern-day scientific article, and in it Alhazen promotes an experimental approach. He was also interested in physics, math, and astronomy, but only 60 of his works have survived. Alhazen coached his students to think for themselves and to combine abstract ideas with real experiments.

## BIOGRAPHY

**BORN**
965 A.D., in Basra (Iraq)

**DIED**
1039 A.D., in Cairo (Egypt)

**FIELD**
mathematics, physics, astronomy

## APPLICATIONS

Alhazen showed how beams of light reflect one another, diffract, and refract. He also did away with the idea that the eye itself emitted images.

## FREEDOM FEIGNER

Alhazen pretended to be mentally ill in order to evade powerful men who wanted him to work for them. He had to flee both the governor of his home region, Basra, as well as the caliph of Cairo.

## INFLUENCES

The caliphs of Cairo wanted their city to be more famous than Baghdad, so they created the House of Wisdom, which taught scholars from across the Arab-Muslim empire.

## CLAIRVOYANT

Alhazen tricked the caliph of Cairo, who wanted to stop the Nile from flooding, by arguing that if the genius minds who built the pyramids couldn't find a solution, then neither could he!

## SUN SPECIALIST

Alhazen explained how a star's radiation gets bigger and smaller because of a phenomenon called refraction.

## FAMOUS FOR

his descriptions of the anatomy of the eye and how vision works

## A GOOD EYE

Alhazen described what happens when light reaches the eye.

## ASTROLABE

Alhazen used an instrument called an astrolabe. It was an Arab invention used to help astronomers measure positions of stars and planets in the night sky.

# The luminary

# Roger Bacon

## APPLICATIONS

Bacon paved the way for the invention of the telescope when he made lenses that would sharpen and magnify the appearance of blurry, distant objects.

## SCANDAL

Without informing his superiors, Bacon contacted the pope, sent him his books, and implored him to reform the education system. As a result, Bacon was banished from his monastery and imprisoned. Deprived of the use of his tools, Bacon wrote a memoir.

**Roger Bacon was a Franciscan monk who was also a philosopher, scientist, and scholar.** Bacon disagreed with the Aristotelian philosophy of the time, which had become mainstream in the Middle Ages with the spread of Christianity. He felt that it was particularly ignorant of the sciences. He used his skills as a talented speaker to promote modern scientific methodology in Europe for the first time. His students called him "Dr. Mirabilis," meaning "wonderful teacher."

## BIOGRAPHY

**BORN**
1214, in Ilchester (England)

**DIED**
1292, in Oxford (England)

**FAMILY**
father was a landowner

**FIELD**
philosophy, mathematics, physics

## INFLUENCES

In Europe, the study of science had stagnated. So Bacon learned many languages to enable him to read texts from antiquity and those written by Jewish, Arab, and Persian scholars.

## FOR LOVE OF KNOWLEDGE

Neighbors in Bacon's village accused him of being a wizard and broke into his observatory and stole his instruments. After the raid, he said: "Many secrets of art and nature are thought by the unlearned to be magical."

## GLASSES

Worn for the first time in the 13th century, they were possibly invented by Bacon.

## RAINBOW

Bacon explained how rainbows are caused by light being refracted when shining through droplets of water.

## DIVING SUIT OR SUBMARINE?

Bacon dreamed of a machine that could explore the deep seas.

**FAMOUS FOR** promoting the scientific method of experimentation

# Ahead of his time

# Nicolaus Copernicus

Copernicus was quite literally a revolutionary. He finally disproved the idea that the Earth stood motionless at the center of the universe (a theory supported by the idea that the world was created by God, for mankind). He knew the scandal he would cause if he announced that the Earth was a satellite that orbits the sun, so he worked quietly on his theory—as he didn't yet have proof—and paved the way for others who followed him.

**AMAZING**

Endlessly editing his book on heliocentrism, finally in 1543 Copernicus decided to publish it, only to die immediately after!

"For who would place this lamp in another or better place than this from which it can illuminate everything at the same time?"

## BIOGRAPHY

**BORN**
1473, Toruń (Prussia, today's Poland)

**DIED**
1543, Frombork (Prussia)

**FAMILY**
adopted by his uncle, a bishop

**FIELD**
theology, mathematics, astronomy

## GEOCENTRISM

Copernicus revised the geocentric model of the universe, which placed the Earth at its center, as proposed by the Greeks Aristotle and Ptolemy.

## "THE COPERNICAN REVOLUTION"

This expression, since passed into everyday use, describes how Copernicus's theory revolutionized the way humans perceive the world. His theory is an example of a paradigm shift—a break with the past.

**11 MINUTES, 14 SECONDS TOO LONG !**

Copernicus calculated that since antiquity, we had mistaken the length of a year.

**REVOLUTIONARY**

His model of the sun at the center of the universe was the first of its kind.

**A POLYMATH**

Copernicus was a member of the clergy and a student of both medicine and law.

**FAMOUS FOR**
his theory of heliocentrism— the sun is the center of the universe

# The quiet revolutionary

# Galileo Galilei

**BIOGRAPHY**

**BORN**
1564, in Pisa (Italy)

**DIED**
1642, in Arcetri (Italy)

**FAMILY**
father was a famous composer

**FIELD**
physics, astronomy, mathematics

**For a long time, life was good for Galileo.** He was born into a famous family, and as a friend of the pope, he was one of the Republic of Venice's protégés. But things went wrong for Galileo when he insisted, like Copernicus, that the Earth travels around the sun. This attracted the wrath of the Church, who forced Galileo to face trial by the formidable Roman Inquisition. Today he is celebrated as a father of modern science for his use of mathematics in demonstrating the truth.

## AMAZING

Legend has it that even when forced to explain his theory at his tribunal, Galileo couldn't help himself but say: "And yet it moves!"

## THE ROMAN INQUISITION

In 1600, another heliocentric named Giordano Bruno was burned at the stake for his theories. Galileo's troubles began ten years later and would continue for 20.

## SCANDAL!

The Church accepted Galileo's theory as a *possible* version of events, but they wouldn't accept that it was the sole truth. And, in order to reach a wider audience, Galileo broke even more rules and wrote in Italian, not Latin!

*"The Book of Nature* is written in the language of mathematics."

**FAMOUS FOR**
defending the heliocentric model of the universe

**TELESCOPE**
Galileo perfected a telescope that could magnify up to 30 times.

**OBSERVATIONS**
Galileo observed craters on the surface of the moon, sunspots, the moons of Jupiter, and the rings of Saturn.

**INQUISITION**
Galileo's sentence was printed and pasted up in universities as a warning, while heliocentrism was banned.

*The stargazer*

# Johannes Kepler

**3**

The first of Kepler's three planetary laws describes how planets move in elliptical orbits, with the sun at the center.

Kepler couldn't choose between theology and astronomy for many years, but after being taught by Tycho Brahe, he decided to stick to astronomy. Brahe had been the astronomer for the emperor of Prague. When Brahe died, Kepler inherited his observatory, books, and notes, and it was with this equipment that he observed how the orbit of the Earth and planets around the sun was not a circle but actually an oval shape, called an ellipse.

## TYCHO BRAHE

Working together in Brahe's observatory, Kepler was inspired by his teacher's interest in the planet Mars. It was while observing Mars that Kepler made his major breakthrough.

## APPLICATIONS

Kepler's laws of planetary motion inspired Isaac Newton and are still used today by engineers when calculating orbits to send satellites into outer space.

## WAR AND EXILE

As a Protestant, Kepler had been forced to move around in order to flee religious tensions. Kepler died during the gruesome Thirty Years' War, when he was on the road to exile in Regensburg, in Germany.

## SNOWFLAKES

Kepler studied the shape and crystal formation of snowflakes.

## FAMOUS FOR
his three laws and his planetary tables

## HIS OBSERVATORY

Kepler had the best equipment in Europe.

## ASTROLOGY

Like many astronomers, Kepler practiced astrology for his patrons.

# The orbit expert

# Isaac Newton

**BIOGRAPHY**

**BORN**
1643, in Woolsthorpe Manor (Great Britain)

**DIED**
1727, in London (Great Britain)

**FAMILY**
father was a landowner

**FIELD**
astronomy, physics, mathematics

**One of the greats,** Newton understood universal gravitation (gravity) and used it to explain the motion of the planets and the sun. Newton also discovered the color spectrum, and did well in math, theology, and alchemy. He died at 85, which for the era in which he lived was very old. During his later years, he had become noticeably bad-tempered and even delusional, which people believe is due to mercury poisoning.

"If I have seen further, it is by standing on the shoulders of giants."

## APPLICATIONS

The sun and the Earth are attracted to one another, but the size of the sun means that it isn't affected by the Earth's pull. The Earth, however, is pulled into the sun's orbit by gravity.

## COLORS

Ever since antiquity, it was thought that sunlight was white, but Newton's famous discovery proved that sunlight is actually composed of all the colors of the rainbow.

## UNIVERSAL GRAVITATION

On our planet, when an object "falls," it is in fact attracted by a downward force called gravity. Newton observed that a falling apple does not fall, but rather, the Earth attracts it.

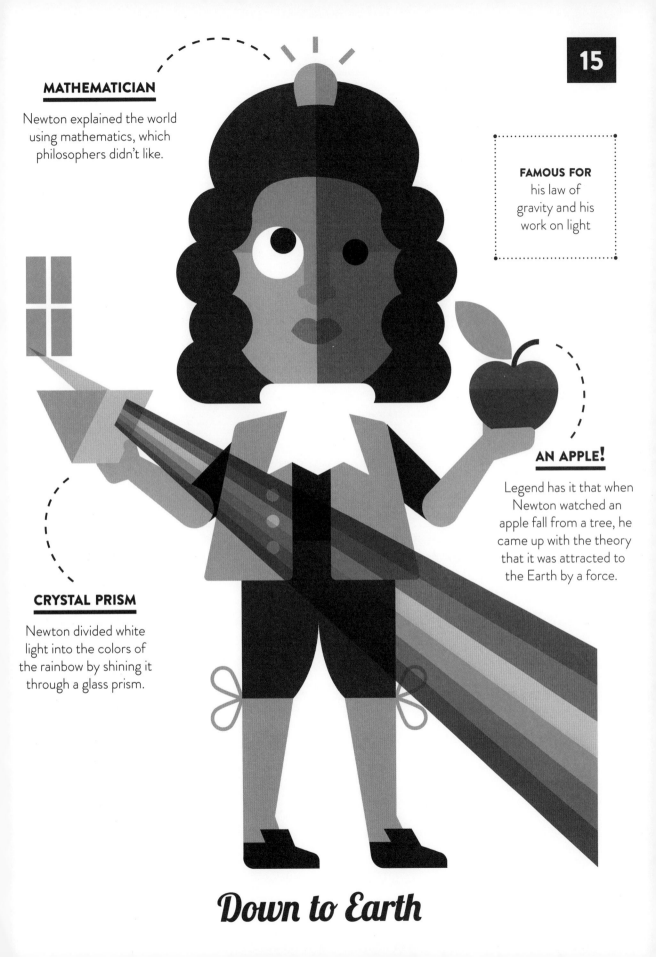

## MATHEMATICIAN

Newton explained the world using mathematics, which philosophers didn't like.

**FAMOUS FOR**
his law of gravity and his work on light

## AN APPLE!

Legend has it that when Newton watched an apple fall from a tree, he came up with the theory that it was attracted to the Earth by a force.

## CRYSTAL PRISM

Newton divided white light into the colors of the rainbow by shining it through a glass prism.

# Down to Earth

# William Harvey

**OPPOSITION**

Guy Patin, dean of the College de France, strongly opposed Harvey. Patin was also the inspiration for Molière's ignorant doctor character in his ballet-opera *The Imaginary Invalid*.

**CONTEXT**

Since antiquity, it was thought that veins and arteries comprised two separate systems, and that the liver was the body's main motor.

**William Harvey was the royal doctor to the Stuarts. One day he shouted, "It flows!"** He had just discovered how blood moves around the body. He performed dissections, which helped him carefully describe how blood is pumped by the heart around a closed circuit in the body, through arteries and veins. He also studied how babies develop from eggs, kick-starting the field of embryology. Like many scientists, Harvey had to battle against tradition to have his ideas recognized.

**BIOGRAPHY**

**BORN**
1578, in Folkestone (Great Britain)

**DIED**
1657, in Roehampton (Great Britain)

**FAMILY**
father was a landowner

**FIELD**
medicine

## ALL IS FROM AN EGG

Harvey concluded that more or less every living organism comes from an egg, and that it is inside the egg that living things form. Before Harvey's time, it was thought that pregnant women sheltered a "homunculus," a full human in miniature form.

## SOLITUDE

During the English Civil War, Harvey's house was targeted and his manuscripts were destroyed by parliamentary supporters. Soon after the war ended, Harvey retired and spent his last years reading.

**EMBRYO**

Harvey thought all life came from an egg.

**FAMOUS FOR**
explaining blood circulation and founding embryology

**STONEHENGE**

Harvey excavated the famous Neolithic site looking for human remains.

**DISSECTION**

As part of his research, Harvey dissected over 40 dead bodies: many were executed criminals, but he also used his father and sister.

# The blood brother

# René Descartes

## BIOGRAPHY

**BORN**
1596, in La Haye en Touraine (France)

**DIED**
1650, in Stockholm (Sweden)

**FAMILY**
father was a politician

**FIELD**
mathematics, physics, philosophy

In his book *Discourse on the Method*, Descartes outlined the four steps that must be followed in order to think correctly. To illustrate the effectiveness of his argument, the philosopher concluded the text with a list of his own scientific discoveries deduced from reasoning. In particular, Descartes is recognized for his important theory about light and his invention of the mathematical concepts of the X and Y axes.

## APPLICATIONS

The word "Cartesian" means of or relating to Descartes. It is used to mean sensible, rigorous, and without imagination. "Cartesianism" is a way of thinking.

"I think therefore I am."

## DOUBT EVERYTHING

What others say can be false. Dreams and optical illusions show that what we see is sometimes not reliable either. Descartes thought that everything we think to be true is actually false, and invented by an "evil demon."

## REASONABLE

Descartes said that the only thing that we cannot doubt is that we can doubt. When Descartes realized that if to doubt is to think, he said his famous line, "I think therefore I am." His goal was to make humans the masters of nature through the power of reason.

**"COGITO ERGO SUM"**

This is Latin for "I think therefore I am." Descartes used both French and Latin formulations of his theory when speaking in public.

**FAMOUS FOR**
writing
*Discourse on the Method*

**THE FIRST DOUBT**

Descartes's work is considered the basis of modern philosophy.

**OF GOOD STOCK**

Descartes was born into a well-known family and Queen Christine of Sweden invited him to her court.

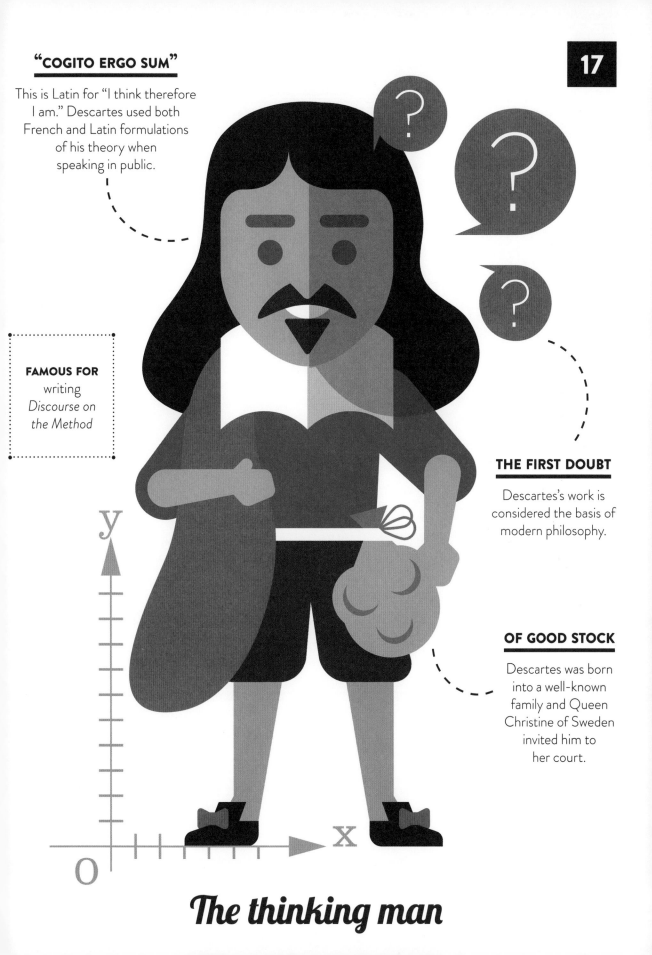

# The thinking man

# Antoine Lavoisier

**Alongside his wife, Anne-Marie, Antoine Lavoisier modernized chemistry.** He showed how combustion is a reaction between a substance and oxygen, and therefore proved that breathing is a form of combustion. Lavoisier also invented chemical equations, found out which chemicals make water and oxygen, and proved that in a chemical reaction no mass is lost. His research marked an end to the mysticism of alchemy. He also had a successful career as a politician!

## TEAMWORK

Joseph Priestley describes several experiments using air, but he never succeeds in naming it. Inspired by Priestley's writings, Lavoisier invents the name "oxygen."

## BIOGRAPHY

**BORN**
1743, in Paris (France)

**DIED**
1794, in Paris (France)

**FAMILY**
father was a politician

**FIELD**
chemistry, philosophy, economics, governance

## MASS

"Nothing is lost, nothing is created, everything is transformed," wrote Lavoisier, following an experiment that burnt tin in air. He discovered that the mass of the product was equal to the mass of the tin and the air at the beginning.

## ELEMENTAL

Lavoisier modernized our understanding of elements. He explained that an element is a material that can't be broken down further. He explained that substances like water were made up of several elements.

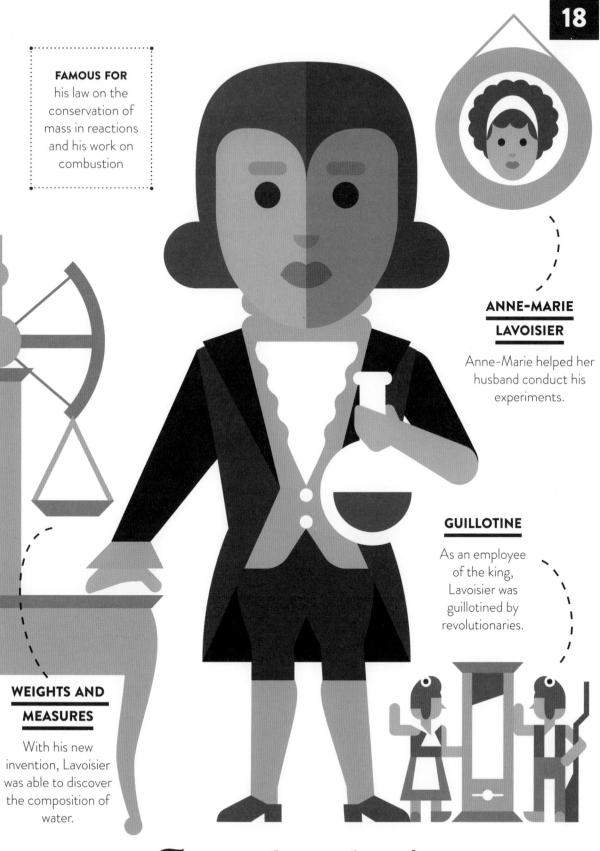

**FAMOUS FOR**
his law on the conservation of mass in reactions and his work on combustion

**ANNE-MARIE LAVOISIER**

Anne-Marie helped her husband conduct his experiments.

**GUILLOTINE**

As an employee of the king, Lavoisier was guillotined by revolutionaries.

**WEIGHTS AND MEASURES**

With his new invention, Lavoisier was able to discover the composition of water.

# The modern chemist

# Mary Anning

## BIOGRAPHY

**BORN**
1799, in Lyme Regis (Great Britain)

**DIED**
1847, in Lyme Regis (Great Britain)

**FAMILY**
orphaned

**FIELD**
paleontology

**One of a handful of amateur scientists who advanced science,** Mary Anning must not be forgotten. She was an orphan and survived by collecting fossils on the beaches of Lyme Regis, on the south coast, and selling them to tourists. When Anning found a rare fossil of a marine reptile called a "plesiosaur," she helped prove a vital argument that explained how living things had evolved. Dinosaur specialists, or paleontologists, see Anning's discoveries as very important and call her the "fossil hunter."

## CONTEXT

During Anning's time, most thought that human beings were created by God in their finished form.

## THE UNKNOWNS

Charles Darwin is well known to have discovered evolution, but he used the findings of people like Anning to help his discoveries. How many other amateur scientists across history went without recognition?

## DATING THE PAST

Scientists began to give dates to rocks and fossils after the discovery of uranium in all living things. Uranium deteriorates over time, so the amount of uranium still in the rock tells us how old it is.

## APPLICATIONS

Anning's plesiosaur is proof of evolution. Although for many years scientists were not able to date her fossil, we now know it to be from the Mesozoic era.

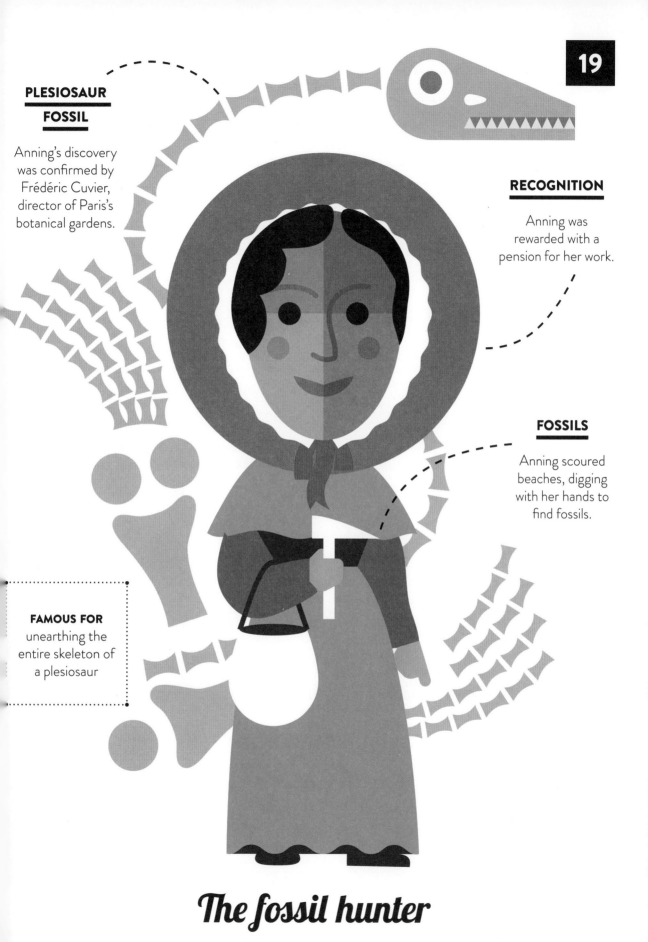

**PLESIOSAUR FOSSIL**

Anning's discovery was confirmed by Frédéric Cuvier, director of Paris's botanical gardens.

**RECOGNITION**

Anning was rewarded with a pension for her work.

**FOSSILS**

Anning scoured beaches, digging with her hands to find fossils.

**FAMOUS FOR**
unearthing the entire skeleton of a plesiosaur

# The fossil hunter

# Michael Faraday

**Faraday secured his position as a super scientist** when he transformed motion into electricity. Although it was known that electricity created a magnetic field, no one understood why motion created electricity. All that changed when Faraday experimented with wrapping two wires around an iron ring and he discovered "electromagnetic induction." His successful tying together of movement, magnetism, and electricity earned him enormous respect, as well as a job teaching at the University of Oxford.

## INFLUENCES

In 1821, Hans Christian Oersted noticed that electricity produces an magnetic field. Inspired by Oersted, Faraday had the idea of linking this to movement.

## CONTEXT

Faraday's work on electricity signaled the end for steam- and coal-powered engines. His discovery paved the way for electrical generators.

## BIOGRAPHY

**BORN**
1791, in London (Great Britain)

**DIED**
1867, in London (Great Britain)

**FAMILY**
father was a blacksmith

**FIELD**
physics and chemistry

## AUTODIDACT

At 14, Faraday became an apprentice bookseller and avid reader. He then assisted the English chemist Humphry Davy, who was working on batteries. This led him to be hired by the English academy of sciences.

## MOONLIGHT CHEMIST

Faraday also discovered that an element called red benzene transformed chlorine gas into a liquid, created optical glasses, and wrote chemistry textbooks!

**ELECTROMAGNETISM**

Faraday discovered electromagnetism.

**FARADAY CAGE**

Another of Faraday's inventions protected scientists against electric shocks.

**BUNSEN BURNER**

Faraday invented the Bunsen burner, still used in chemistry labs.

**FAMOUS FOR**
discovering electromagnetic induction

# The electromaniac

# James Clerk Maxwell

## BIOGRAPHY

**BORN**
1831, in Edinburgh (Scotland)

**DIED**
1879, in Cambridge (Great Britain)

**FAMILY**
father was a landowner

**FIELD**
mathematics and physics

**The late great Maxwell observed how light waves and electric waves move at the same speed.** This made him realize that light is both electric and magnetic. He went on to explain the existence of "electromagnetic" waves. Maxwell also explained the three categories of light: colors that are visible, and infrared and ultraviolet, which are invisible to the naked eye. He is also famous for studying how the colored rings around Saturn are made.

## MISUNDERSTOOD

Maxwell shocked people when he said that light waves and electromagnetic waves were of the same nature. He wasn't discouraged and wrote about it in his famous "Maxwell's equations."

## INTERACTIONS

Faraday discovered the existence of electromagnetism but he wasn't able to take it much further. He spoke with Maxwell, who took up the challenge and was able to show how electric currents and magnetic fields interact.

## APPLICATIONS

In 1888, Heinrich Rudolf Hertz proved that electromagnetic waves were capable of traveling through walls. This paved the way for the invention of the radio.

> "I stand not on the shoulders of Newton, but on the shoulders of James Clerk Maxwell."
> Albert Einstein

## 21

**RADIO**

Radios and cell phones work because of electromagnetic waves.

**VOYAGER 1**

In 1980, when Voyager 1 flew by Saturn, Maxwell's theories were proven correct.

**INSTRUMENTS OF EXPLORATION**

His equations enabled the invention of instruments of exploration, both big and small.

**FAMOUS FOR**
changing how we understand electricity, magnetism, and light

# The scientist who made waves

# Charles Darwin

**BIOGRAPHY**

**BORN**
1809, in Shrewsbury (Great Britain)

**DIED**
1882, in Down House (Great Britain)

**FAMILY**
father was a doctor

**FIELD**
zoology and biology

**Much like Copernicus during the Renaissance, Darwin transformed how we perceive the world** when he contradicted the biblical account of mankind's creation by God and argued that ever since life appeared on Earth it has slowly transformed over time. Darwin went further still when he claimed that humans and monkeys share a common ancestor. But, while the world of science rejoiced in his revolutionary theory, the Church and a large section of society declared war on his ideas.

**AMAZING**
Darwin was so lazy at school that his father said to him: "You care for nothing but shooting, dogs and rat-catching, and you will be a disgrace to yourself and all your family."

## HUMANITY: A SPECIAL CASE

Darwin claimed that humankind's powers of thought and morality have had a stronger effect on our evolution than even the laws of natural selection.

## NATURAL SELECTION

In any species, the individuals who adapted best survived to have babies, who would in turn survive well like their parents. This causes tansformation of the species to be very slow. It eliminates the weak in a process called natural selection.

**APPLICATIONS**
Like two branches that grow from a single tree, humans and monkeys grew from a common ancestor. This idea was scandalous at the time but now we know it is true.

## 22

**OBSERVATIONS**

Darwin founded ethology, which is the observation of animal behaviors.

**FAMOUS FOR**
his theory of the evolution of the species

**HMS *BEAGLE***

Darwin traveled the world for five years by boat, studying nature across America and the Pacific, which he would later use for his theory.

**THE GALAPAGOS**

Darwin deduced that the 13 species of chaffinch he observed there all shared a common ancestor.

# The evolutionary revolutionary

# Gregor Mendel

**BIOGRAPHY**

**BORN**
1822, in Heinzendorf, Moravia (Austria-Hungary)

**DIED**
1884, in Brno (Czech Republic)

**FAMILY**
parents were farmers

**FIELD**
botany and biology

**APPLICATIONS**

Mendel would never know how inherited characteristics are in fact determined by "genes," which are expressed or not expressed, or mutate.

**With his experiments on pea plants, Mendel was able to figure out how they inherited characteristics, such as seed shape, flower color, and whether they are smooth, ridged, yellow, or green-tinted.** He was surprised by his results and he interpreted his findings using a new type of math called "statistics." This helped him understand how two parents pass certain traits on to their children. Mendel's work went largely unnoticed, but he knew that what he had discovered was important. It turned out that Mendel really was onto something...

## ¾ - ¼

Mendel crossed smooth peas with ridged peas. In the 1st generation, they were all smooth, but in the 2nd, ¾ of peas were smooth and ¼ were ridged!

## THE IDEA

A recessive trait is overtaken by a dominant one. In the first generation of peas, the dominant smooth trait masked the recessive ridged one. When ridges reappeared in the second generation of peas, Mendel used statistics to explain.

## LAWS OF INHERITANCE

Mendel didn't realize that his discoveries about peas actually applied to all living things. Eye and hair color depend on a pair of characteristics (recessive or dominant) called a "hereditary particularity."

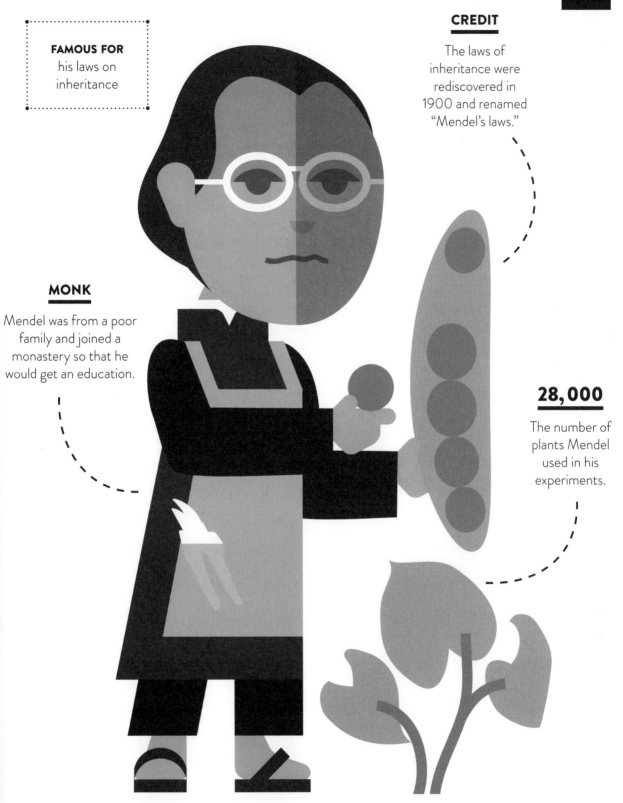

his laws on
inheritance

**CREDIT**

The laws of
inheritance were
rediscovered in
1900 and renamed
"Mendel's laws."

**MONK**

Mendel was from a poor
family and joined a
monastery so that he
would get an education.

**28,000**

The number of
plants Mendel
used in his
experiments.

## The inheritance innovator

# Louis *Pasteur*

If a surgeon washes their hands before operating, the rate of hospital deaths is reduced by half.

## OPPOSITION

The doctor Félix-Archimède Pouchet said that life could just spring from nowhere, without reason. Pasteur disproved this theory by explaining the actions of microbes.

**Pasteur invented the practice of microbiology and changed medicine forever.** He suspected that when things rotted, they were reacting with germs, or "microbes." He thought these microbes were responsible for illnesses too. He developed vaccination injections that stop people from catching disease. This invention changed everything. Pasteur successfully vaccinated a child who had been bitten 14 times by an animal infected with rabies.

## BIOGRAPHY

**BORN**
1822, in Dole (France)

**DIED**
1895, in Marnes-la-Coquette (France)

**FAMILY**
father was an artisan

**FIELD**
chemistry, biology

## TO THE RESCUE

Governments, companies, farmers, and industries all asked Pasteur to work for them, which is how he came to study germs and diseases in winemaking, vinegar, beer, silkworms, and hens...

## VACCINATION

The practice of vaccination (safely introducing the body to a disease) had long been used by the Chinese and the scientist Edward Jenner. But it was Pasteur who modernized it and identified different types of germs, in particular the virus that causes rabies.

## 24

## THE PASTEUR INSTITUTE

In the 21st century, the battle against disease is still being fought here.

**FAMOUS FOR** uncovering the movement of microbes and modernizing vaccination

## PASTEURIZATION

Pasteurization uses heat to kill off germs, which makes food safe.

## WASH YOUR HANDS

Pasteur recommended hand-washing in order to destroy germs, but for many years doctors were slow to change.

# The diligent do-gooder

# Dmitri Ivanovich Mendeleev

**BIOGRAPHY**

**BORN**
1834, in Tobolsk (Russia)

**DIED**
1907, in St. Petersburg (Russia)

**FAMILY**
parents were glass merchants

**FIELD**
chemistry

**Mendeleev invented the periodic table. This table arranges all of the elements in a grid according to their properties.** An element is a solid, liquid, or gas that cannot be divided into any smaller parts. Mendeleev figured out that all elements differed according to the structure of its nucleus. From here, he drew up a simple table, like an alphabet for chemists, containing 63 elements. He made sure that the table could grow to fit more elements, which was clever thinking, as in 2016, the 118th element was added!

## CONTEXT

The invention of machines fueled by coal, gas, and electricity led to the industrial revolution in the 19th century—evidence of how important science is to advancing the lives of all!

## ANTICIPATION

Using the ideas he developed, and noticing specific gaps in his table, Mendeleev predicted that there were still more elements to be discovered or artificially made.

## CLASSIFICATION

Mendeleev grouped elements together into families according to similar properties. Then he could figure out how their properties related to the makeup of their protons and neutrons.

## APPLICATIONS

There are 92 natural elements, but there are also some that only humans can make.

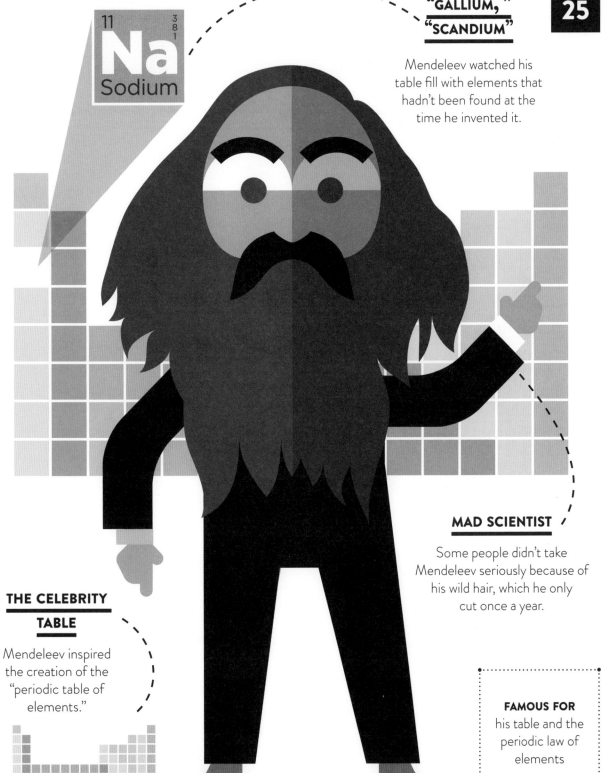

## 25

11 3 8 1
**Na**
Sodium

"GALLIUM,"
"SCANDIUM"

Mendeleev watched his table fill with elements that hadn't been found at the time he invented it.

**MAD SCIENTIST**

Some people didn't take Mendeleev seriously because of his wild hair, which he only cut once a year.

**THE CELEBRITY TABLE**

Mendeleev inspired the creation of the "periodic table of elements."

**FAMOUS FOR**
his table and the periodic law of elements

# The organizer

# Ada Lovelace

Ada Lovelace was the first mathematician to fully understand the potential of the inventor Charles Babbage's mechanical computer. She wrote specific instructions for the computer, which we would now call algorithms. Lovelace's father was the tortured Romantic poet Lord Byron. Lovelace was encouraged by her mother to study scientific subjects in order to be different from her father. Mission accomplished!

## BIOGRAPHY

**BORN**
1815, in London (Great Britain)

**DIED**
1852, in London (Great Britain)

**FAMILY**
father was a writer, mother was an intellectual

**FIELD**
mathematics

## CONTEXT
Lovelace lived in an age when rich women were expected to raise children and not to study science!

## MARY SOMERVILLE
The renowned writer Mary Somerville was Lovelace's private tutor. Somerville introduced Lovelace to Babbage, who was a professor of math at the University of Cambridge.

## ADA LOVELACE DAY
On this day in October in the UK, people celebrate women's contributions to science. People also spend this day encouraging young women to get involved in science and math, which are subjects still dominated by men.

## INFLUENCES
Based on the principle of weaving, Babbage's analytic machine received data and instructions using a system of punched cards. Sadly too expensive, this first computer was never manufactured.

## 26

**FAMOUS FOR**
her research into Charles Babbage's "Analytical Engine"

**CHARLES BABBAGE**

She was friends with Charles Babbage and her work enabled him to make major breakthroughs in computing.

**COUNTEREXAMPLE**

Doctors believed that Lovelace's great intelligence came from the cancer that eventually killed her.

**ADA**

The famous computer language ADA was named after Lovelace.

# Queen of Algorithms

# David Hilbert

In 1900, David Hilbert created a puzzle that would cause mathematicians across the world to think and dream (and have nightmares) for years. Hilbert wrote a list of 23 unsolved mathematical problems that if solved would be a huge leap forward in math. Although some remain unsolved, his problems gave shape to a century of research. Hilbert also attempted to link every single branch of math into one big super-theory. He studied many subjects, with over 20 concepts and proofs to his name!

## INFLUENCES

In 2000, inspired by Hilbert's legacy, the Clay Mathematics Institute devised 7 "Millennium Problems," only one of which has been successfully solved!

"We must know—we will know!"
from the epitaph on Hilbert's tomb

## BIOGRAPHY

**BORN**
1862, in Königsberg (Germany)

**DIED**
1943, in Göttingen (Germany)

**FAMILY**
father a civil servant

**FIELD**
mathematics

## TEACHING

Hilbert taught at the University of Göttingen, which was the best in the world at the time, for all of his working life. Under his influence, German research experienced a golden age, which ended when Jewish academics were expelled by the Nazis.

## GOOD QUESTION

Can math always prove what is true and false? Kurt Gödel answered no to this question, posed by Hilbert in 1931. Alan Turing used Gödel's response as the basis for his work on artificial intelligence.

## 27

**FEMINIST?**

Hilbert allowed the female mathematician Emmy Noether to lecture under his name, as she would have been forbidden as a woman otherwise!

**21 SOLVED PROBLEMS**

In 2018, two of Hilbert's problems remain unsolved, while four have only been solved in part.

**POPULAR**

Hilbert's students could purchase postcards that featured Hilbert's photograph.

**FAMOUS FOR** his list of problems and his attempts to unify the branches of mathematics

*david hilbert*

# *1 mathematician, 23 problems*

# Marie Curie

**Marie Curie was born in Poland and traveled to Paris in France to study chemistry, math, and physics.** Curie discovered that there were different types of radioactive materials and studied how they were made. She discovered the radioactive materials polonium and radium. She was the first woman to be made a professor at the Sorbonne University, the first person to receive two Nobel Prizes, and the first to be commemorated in France's Panthéon mausoleum! Despite this, she still had to defend her discoveries to people who didn't believe her.

## CONTEXT

X-rays had just been discovered when Antoine Henri Becquerel noted that uranium emits a different type of ray, charged with energy. Curie then jumped into action!

## PRECIOUS METAL

A group of rich Americans gave Curie one gram of radioactive radium. However, in 1914, as France was threatened by German invasion, the government asked Curie for her radium. She refused and hid her precious treasure.

> "I am among those who think that science has great beauty."

## A FAMILY AFFAIR

Marie and her husband, fellow scientist Pierre Curie, had two daughters. The eldest daughter, Irène, was also a great scientist and was the first to artificially produce radioactivity.

## BIOGRAPHY

**BORN**
1867, in Warsaw (Poland)

**DIED**
1934, in Passy (France)

**FAMILY**
mother was a headteacher, father was a professor of physics and math

**FIELD**
physics

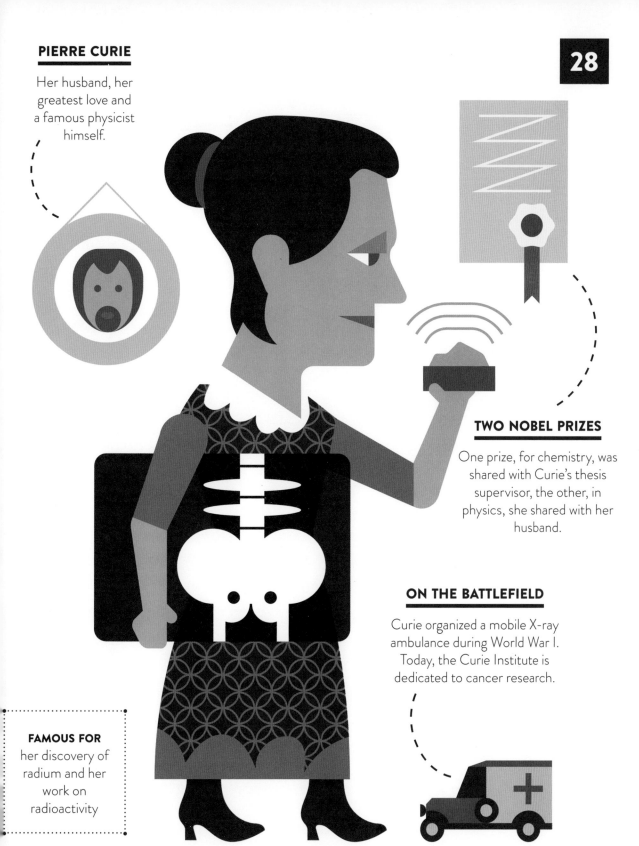

## 28

**PIERRE CURIE**

Her husband, her greatest love and a famous physicist himself.

**TWO NOBEL PRIZES**

One prize, for chemistry, was shared with Curie's thesis supervisor, the other, in physics, she shared with her husband.

**ON THE BATTLEFIELD**

Curie organized a mobile X-ray ambulance during World War I. Today, the Curie Institute is dedicated to cancer research.

**FAMOUS FOR**
her discovery of radium and her work on radioactivity

# Radioactive hero

# Ernest Rutherford

**In 1917, Ernest Rutherford discovered that atoms have a dense center called a nucleus formed of protons and neutrons.** Before that, he had shown how radioactive things such as polonium sent out waves called "radioactivity," which resulted from the breakdown of atoms. Rutherford also performed something called a "transmutation," where he transformed one element into another by changing the protons and neutrons in the atom's nucleus.

### CONTEXT

Rutherford was lucky to study in an era of great discoveries. He first worked on radio waves, before moving on to gases.

### ZOOMING IN

The electron was discovered in 1903, and in 1917 we learned that the nucleus is comprised of protons and neutrons.

### SOLVAY CONFERENCE

At first, Rutherford's model was ignored, but in 1913 at the Solvay Conference, the world's great physicists debated his idea, including Rutherford's academic advisor J. J. Thomson, Marie Curie, and Niels Bohr.

### INFLUENCES

In antiquity, Democritus wrote that everything is made of infinite miniscule particles, which he called "atoms"—the Greek word for "indivisible."

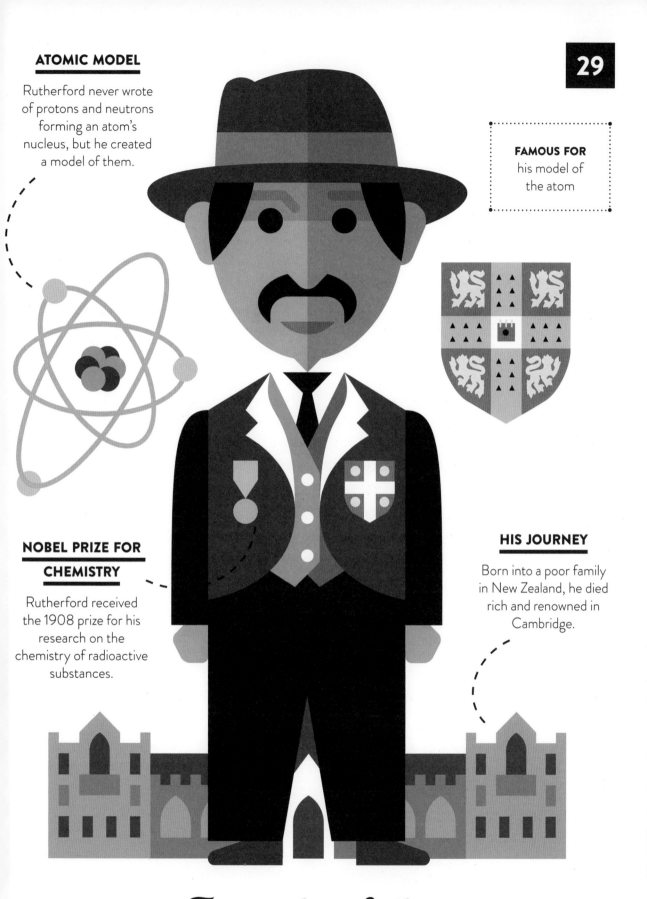

## 29

**ATOMIC MODEL**

Rutherford never wrote of protons and neutrons forming an atom's nucleus, but he created a model of them.

**FAMOUS FOR**
his model of the atom

**NOBEL PRIZE FOR CHEMISTRY**

Rutherford received the 1908 prize for his research on the chemistry of radioactive substances.

**HIS JOURNEY**

Born into a poor family in New Zealand, he died rich and renowned in Cambridge.

# The nuclear father

# Albert Einstein

## 1905

During this "extraordinary year," Einstein published four important scientific papers!

Einstein is one of the most famous scientists ever to have lived. He had so many brilliant ideas but one of his most famous is his equation $E = mc^2$, meaning the mass of an object is equal to its energy. His general theory of relativity became one of the most significant texts about physics in the 19th and 20th centuries. It changed how we think about the universe. Einstein's non-conformism did not stop him from becoming a living legend.

### BIOGRAPHY

**BORN**
1879, in Ulm (Germany)

**DIED**
1955, in Princeton (United States)

**FAMILY**
father a small factory owner

**FIELD**
physics

### APPLICATIONS

The laws of relativity helped scientists to better understand the architecture of the universe, and the nature of stars and galaxies. It also helped people to invent GPS (global positioning system).

### RELATIVITY

Space and time are connected. Two events that appear to occur at the same time and in the same place when viewed from a different location may not appear to be simultaneous—this is the fourth dimension.

### THE ATOMIC BOMB

$E = mc^2$ allowed for the invention of the atom bomb, although Einstein himself did not make it. As the Nazis worked to build an atom bomb, Einstein convinced the US to work on their own to help them win World War II.

## 30

**HIS BRAIN**

After Einstein's death, his brain was stolen and hidden for many years. It was then cut up to try and uncover the secret to his genius!

**THE SUN**

Working on the force of the sun's attraction, Einstein proved his theories of relativity.

$$E=mc^2$$

**FBI FILE**

America was suspicious of Einstein, a socialist, pacifist, anti-racist immigrant—his FBI file was 1,800 pages long.

FBI SECURITY

FBI SECURITY

**FAMOUS FOR**
his laws of relativity and $E = mc^2$, the most famous equation in the world

# The genius

# Niels *Bohr*

## BIOGRAPHY

**BORN**
1885, in Copenhagen (Denmark)

**DIED**
1962, in Copenhagen (Denmark)

**FAMILY**
father was a professor of medicine

**FIELD**
physics

**Niels Bohr came up with the idea that electrons inside an atom change according to the path they take to travel around the nucleus of the atom.** This was the key idea that led to quantum physics, which was one of the major breakthroughs of the 20th century. It allowed exploration of infinitely small things. Despite the chaos of World War II, research into quantum mechanics continued internationally. This research has enabled the world of technology we now live in.

## APPLICATIONS

Every day we use technologies that deploy quantum mechanics: LED lamps, USB sticks, transistors, computers, and cell phones.

## THE MISSING LINK

How does Einstein's theory of general relativity relate to the laws of quantum physics? This question still hasn't been answered to this day.

## DISTURBING

A quantum particle behaves very strangely indeed. Although it occupies as much space as possible, as soon as we try to measure it, it shrinks—sort of like a cloud that disappears once you are inside it!

## OPPOSITION

Einstein hated the uncertainty of quantum mechanics: "God doesn't play dice with the universe." To which Bohr replied: "Einstein, don't tell God what to do."

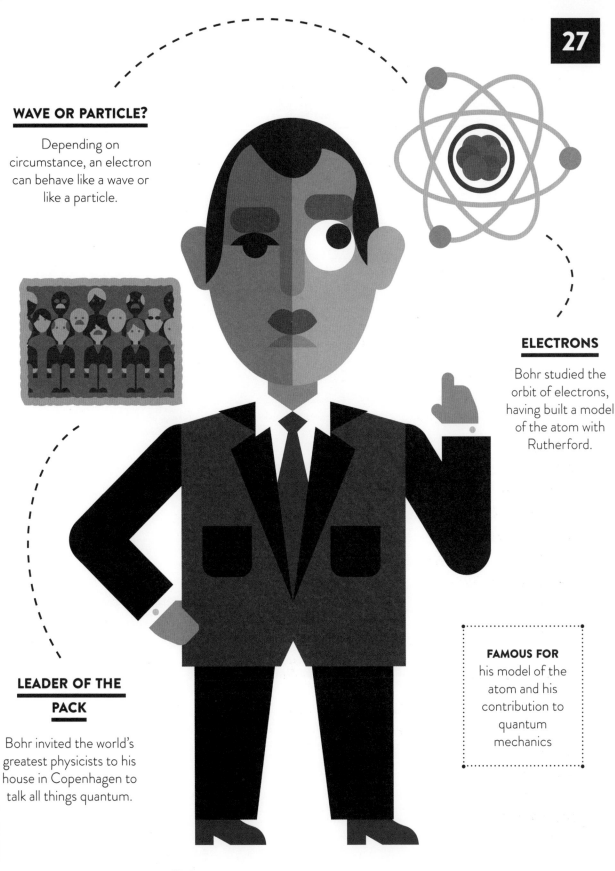

**WAVE OR PARTICLE?**

Depending on circumstance, an electron can behave like a wave or like a particle.

**ELECTRONS**

Bohr studied the orbit of electrons, having built a model of the atom with Rutherford.

**LEADER OF THE PACK**

Bohr invited the world's greatest physicists to his house in Copenhagen to talk all things quantum.

**FAMOUS FOR**
his model of the atom and his contribution to quantum mechanics

# The quantum whizz

# Alfred Wegener

## BIOGRAPHY

**BORN**
1880, in Berlin
(Germany)

**DIED**
1930, in Greenland

**FAMILY**
father was a
clergyman

**FIELD**
meteorology,
astronomy

**In 1915, Wegener became interested in geology and geophysics.** He was brave enough to suggest that, thousands of years ago, the Earth was made up of only one continent called Pangea, and that our six continents were created when this super continent broke apart. He argued that continents are always moving slowly, a few centimeters per year. Today, we know Wegener was correct, but unfortunately he wasn't listened to at the time!

## CONTEXT

It used to be thought that the Earth's continents were once joined together by bridges that had fallen down and made way for oceans.

## COAST TO COAST

The most striking evidence for Wegener's theory is how the coasts of the continents fit together like a jigsaw puzzle. He explained that his idea of "drifting" continents came from observing ice floes break up at the North Pole.

## "PLATE TECTONICS"

Wegener's theory was renamed "plate tectonics" when, during the 1960s, deep-sea exploration allowed scientists to understand how and why the continents drifted apart.

## OPPOSITION

Wegener had scraps of evidence that supported his theory, but no model. The mathematician Harold Jeffreys refuted Wegener's idea using calculations.

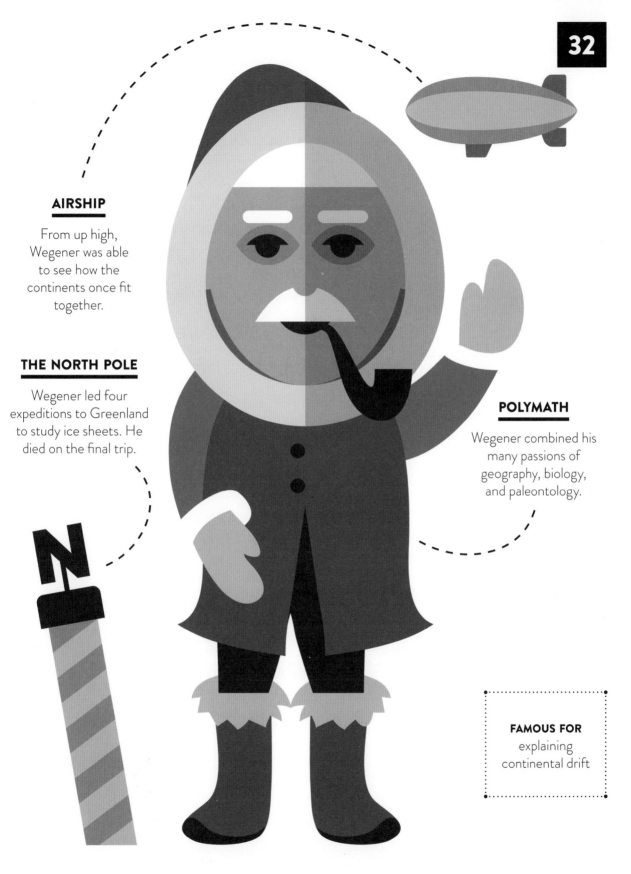

## 32

## AIRSHIP

From up high, Wegener was able to see how the continents once fit together.

## THE NORTH POLE

Wegener led four expeditions to Greenland to study ice sheets. He died on the final trip.

## POLYMATH

Wegener combined his many passions of geography, biology, and paleontology.

**FAMOUS FOR**
explaining
continental drift

# The tectonic explorer

# Alan Turing

## BIOGRAPHY

**BORN**
1912, in London
(Great Britain)

**DIED**
1954, in Cheshire
(Great Britain)

**FAMILY**
father was an army
officer

**FIELD**
mathematics

**Alan Turing won World War II (sort of).** He worked for the British secret service and accomplished mission Ultra. Its objective? To devise a way of decoding the Nazis' messages that were encrypted using their Enigma machine. Having proved how anything that has been "computed" can be broken down step by step, Turing eventually cracked the Nazis' code, aided by almost *all* of Oxford's and Cambridge's mathematics students. After the war, he went on to invent the first computer.

## APPLICATION

Encode = transform letters into numbers. Decode = turn the numbers back into letters.

## A WAR OF NUMBERS

Poland never succeeded in decoding Enigma, which the Nazis had perfected. They turned to Britain for help, who at first hired 10 people, including 2 mathematicians, but the team eventually grew to 10,000 code crackers.

## PERSECUTED

Turing was gay at a time when the law still considered it a crime. Charged in court, he was forced to undergo treatment that made him depressed. It isn't clear whether he committed suicide or was assassinated.

## CONTEXT

By 1940, Hitler had invaded almost all of Europe apart from Britain. "Ultra" would try to decode messages exchanged between the German commanders and their submarines.

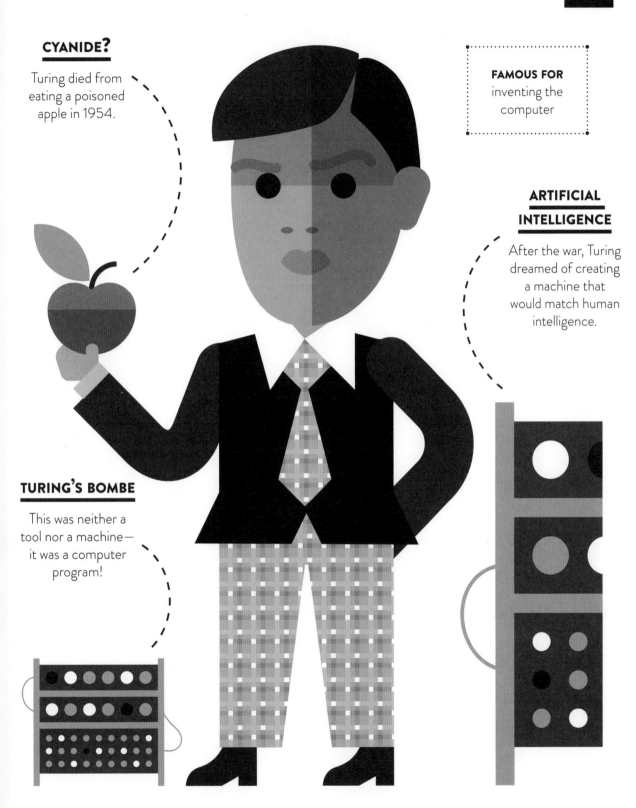

## 33

**CYANIDE?**
Turing died from eating a poisoned apple in 1954.

**FAMOUS FOR**
inventing the computer

**ARTIFICIAL INTELLIGENCE**
After the war, Turing dreamed of creating a machine that would match human intelligence.

**TURING'S BOMBE**
This was neither a tool nor a machine—it was a computer program!

# Freedom and information

# Rosalind Franklin

## BIOGRAPHY

**BORN**
1920, in London
(Great Britain)

**DIED**
1958, in London
(Great Britain)

**FAMILY**
father was a
merchant banker

**FIELD**
biology

**Franklin and her laboratory colleague Maurice Wilkins didn't get along.** She found a new job in another lab, where she wanted to publish her photographs that revealed the structure of DNA. Unluckily for Franklin, Wilkins had already shown her amazing photographs to two scientists, Watson and Crick, who were also working on a DNA model, and the images confirmed their theory. Watson, Crick, and Wilkins published their paper without Franklin, and when in 1962 the trio received the Nobel Prize for Medicine, Franklin had already died of cancer.

## APPLICATIONS

It was thought that DNA was made of strands of bricks, but this didn't explain how the strands were linked. The double helix shape revealed how to decode human genetics.

## THE HIGHEST FORM OF RECOGNITION

Many thinkers and researchers never receive the recognition they deserve. For example, in the sciences, fewer than 20 women have received the Nobel Prize, while more than 600 men have.

## THE PHOTO

"The instant I saw the photograph my mouth fell open and my pulse began to race," recounted Watson, who his colleagues joked had won the Nobel Prize for boringness.

## AMAZING

In a short article, Watson and Crick described the structure of DNA and how genetic inheritance works in all forms of life.

## 34

**DNA**
Franklin played an essential role in the discovery of DNA's structure.

**PHOTO 51**
Franklin took this famous photograph using a technique called X-ray diffraction.

**HER NOTES**
Franklin's writings show that she was considering a helix shape from as early as 1951.

**FAMOUS FOR**
her X-ray photography that showed the shape of DNA

# The unsung hero

# HGP
## and the Human Genome

**CHRONOLOGY**

**1985**
the idea is born

**1990**
project launch

**APRIL 14, 2003**
99.9% of the human genome has been coded

**For 15 years, an international research group worked on the Human Genome Project, or HGP.** The group succeeded in "sequencing" the DNA, or decoding all the chemical instructions that are contained within our genes, which tell our bodies how to work. A rival sequencing project set up by Celera Genomics was established as a private competitor to the publicly funded HGP, intending to sell the sequence first. Luckily for humanity, the human genome could not be legally patented and the HGP won the race!

**APPLICATIONS**

By knowing how to read our genes, we are able to treat certain illnesses, and it also means we can reduce the risk of illnesses developing even in an unborn child.

## GENOME: A DEFINITION

A genome is all the genetic information—known as "genes"—contained within every cell of an organism. DNA is the support material of the genome.

### DATA SHARING

In 1995, the directors of the HGP decided that the data produced on the human genome could not be sold. However, it is still possible to sell its applications.

**TEAMWORK**

In 1998, a team working for a private company announced that they would be able to finish the sequencing in just three years. If they succeeded, they would sell their results.

## THE CODE OF LIFE

It's thanks to the genome that the human body works.

## THE PROPERTY OF HUMANITY

In 1998, it was decided that the components of the genome belong to humanity.

## HGP

The Human Genome Project was born in the USA, but eventually united 350 laboratories from 18 countries.

# The international effort

# Vera Rubin

## BIOGRAPHY

**BORN**
1928, in Philadelphia (United States)

**DIED**
2016, in Princeton (United States)

**FAMILY**
the daughter of two engineers

**FIELD**
astrophysics

**It is thanks to Vera Rubin that astrophysicists have been able to take on one of the most exciting mysteries of our time: the existence of dark matter in the universe.** Rubin noticed that collisions between galaxies showed how the universe's expansion is uneven, meaning our cosmos is not perfectly shaped but is more like a sponge. She spent many years studying her beloved sky, but it would be several decades before Rubin's trailblazing work was taken seriously...

## CONTEXT

In the 20th century, it was discovered that the universe (which we had thought was just one galaxy) was in fact getting bigger and contained many galaxies.

## THE UNIVERSE

The proportion of the universe made up of stars and gas that we can see and observe is just 5%, which means that the 95% of the universe we ignore could be formed of dark matter.

## DARK MATTER?

The movements of some stars at the center of galaxies, such as the Milky Way, cannot be explained by Newton's gravity or Einstein's laws. Instead, Rubin suggested that massive invisible objects might exist and change the way stars move around.

## AMAZING

Rubin built her own telescope at the age of just 10, only to be later told by a university professor: "As long as you stay away from science, you'll be fine!"

## 36

**GAMOW**

Rubin was spotted and then mentored by George Gamow, known for his work on the Big Bang.

**SPIRAL GALAXIES**

Studying the motion of these stars, Rubin noted how they do not obey the established laws of physics.

**A SCIENTIST**

Rubin had to battle to even be considered a scientist!

**FAMOUS FOR** having kicked off research into dark matter and the formation of galaxies

# The pioneer of the universe

# Françoise Barré-Sinoussi

**In 1983, Barré-Sinoussi discovered HIV, the deadly virus that causes AIDS, just as the terrible epidemic was spreading across the globe.** This breakthrough lead to more discoveries, like how HIV is transmitted sexually, from pregnant mother to unborn child, as well as by blood transfusion. Barré-Sinoussi has since worked closely with the countries most affected by the AIDS crisis, while her activism has seen her fight against the spread of the virus and for greater public understanding of it.

## 35 MILLION DEATHS

and around 37 million people are still living with AIDS. Today, in richer countries, infection is controlled through medication, but in poorer countries, still only half of those with the illness are treated.

### APPLICATIONS

Recognizing the HIV virus has enabled the invention of screening tests, while understanding its spread has led to the creation of medicines that can limit it.

## TREATMENT

HIV (human immuno-deficiency virus) infects the cells that defend the body. Without treatment, people who have HIV are less able to fight off illnesses and infections. There is still no vaccine to prevent the disease, but it can be managed.

### CONTEXT

In 1983, the virologist Luc Montagnier was leading a group of lab researchers in the pursuit of a new virus, which would then be detected for the first time by Barré-Sinoussi.

## BIOGRAPHY

**BORN**
1947, in Paris (France)

**FAMILY**
father was a surveyor, mother was a housewife

**FIELD**
biology

## 37

## VIRUS VOCATION

Barré-Sinoussi is a virus specialist: from common colds to AIDS.

## ACTIVISM

Barré-Sinoussi is president of Sidaction, a French charity of researchers, health workers, and HIV-positive activists who aim to increase awareness of the virus and its prevention.

## NOBEL PRIZE

Barré-Sinoussi won the Nobel Prize for Medicine.

**FAMOUS FOR**
discovering the virus that causes AIDS

# The AIDS warrior

# Tim Berners-Lee

**How to help the thousands of researchers** working at CERN (the European Organization for Nuclear Research) efficiently exchange data? In 1989, the physicist Tim Berners-Lee proposed a digital method of linking together documents. When Berners-Lee's software became free and available to all, web navigation took over the world! Since then, Berners-Lee has founded an organization dedicated to advancing and protecting the freedom of the internet.

## APPLICATIONS

We say "go on the internet," but the internet is in fact a computer network that was developed in the 1960s. In reality, it is web technology that allows us to "surf."

## BIOGRAPHY

**BORN**
1955, in London (Grear Britain)

**FAMILY**
the son of two computer scientists

**FIELD**
physics and computer science

## "VAGUE, BUT EXCITING"

Were the words said by Berners-Lee's boss when he was presented with the idea for the internet. In 1991, the internet was made available to the physicists working at CERN. By 2017, it had 3 billion users worldwide.

## $0

Berners-Lee has insisted that the web must always remain free, accessible to all and immune to political or commercial forces.

## SERENDIPITY

The web has made the word "serendipity" fashionable, as it explains the way that we often stumble unexpectedly upon a website while looking for something else on the internet.

## 38

**FAMOUS FOR**
inventing the web

**THE WEB**
The web was first nicknamed "the net."

**'WWW'**
We use an abbreviation of "World Wide Web" at the beginning of all web addresses.

**THE PIONEER OF PROTOCOL**
Berners-Lee invented the URL address, "http" protocol, and a simple form of code called "HTML."

# The internet's inventor

# Stephen *Hawking*

**BIOGRAPHY**

**BORN**
1942, in Oxford
(Great Britain)

**DIED**
2018, in Cambridge
(Great Britain)

**FAMILY**
father was a
biologist; mother
was an Oxford
graduate in politics,
philosophy, and
economics

**FIELD**
physics

**This physicist embodied the idea that science is a question of thought alone.** Hawking was paralyzed by a degenerative illness. In spite of this, his extraordinary intelligence enabled him to ponder the universe and discover something new: that black holes emit particles. His book *A Brief History of Time* fascinated readers and he used his fame to challenge power, arguing with politicians about climate change and the dangers of artificial intelligence.

## 3

According to doctors, Hawking only had three years left to live when he was diagnosed with motor neurone disease at 21. He would actually live for 55 more years.

## HAWKING RADIATION

Using the laws of quantum mechanics, Hawking was the first to propose that because black holes lose mass they must emit radiation and eventually evaporate. This contradicted the general theory of relativity.

## BLACK HOLE

A black hole is an area where gravitation is so intense that no material or light can escape from it. At its center is what's called a "singularity": a place where gravity is infinite and space no longer makes sense.

"People are fascinated by the contrast between my very limited physical powers, and the vast nature of the universe I deal with."

## 39

**BLACK HOLES**

According to Hawking, black holes played a role in the beginnings of the universe.

HAWKING

A brief history of time

**TREKKIE AND SCI-FI FAN**

Hawking has appeared as a character in *Star Trek* and *The Simpsons*.

**FAMOUS FOR** discovering that black holes emit particles

**AGANST ALL ODDS**

Despite his paralysis, Hawking managed to have a family and head a laboratory.

*The brilliant mind*

# Neil deGrasse Tyson

**Director of the famous Hayden Planetarium in New York, Tyson is truly out of this world.** He is an astrophysicist and researcher and has also popularized complex scientific theories and concepts through his use of simple language. Cool yet razor-sharp, Tyson is a regular on television and Twitter. He particularly enjoys sharing his thoughts on his faith in science and his belief that alien life really does exist...

## ON PLUTO

A big debate was ignited when Pluto, long considered one of the nine planets in our solar system, was declassified. Tyson supported the move, arguing that Pluto is indeed a dwarf planet.

## THE BLUE MARBLE

Tyson explained to former US president George W. Bush that space travel gives hope to humankind. It also gives perspective. The Earth from space looks tiny and fragile, and reminds us that we need to look after it.

### INFLUENCES

As a teenager, Tyson met the astronomer turned science journalist Carl Sagan: "That afternoon I learned from Carl the kind of person I wanted to become."

"After we went to the moon, it all ended. We stopped dreaming."

## TV AND FILM CRITIC

The scientific accuracy of both gravity and *Game of Thrones* has been discussed by Tyson on Twitter.

## HONORS

Tyson has received awards from NASA and has an asteroid named after him.

## DIRECTOR OF THE HAYDEN PLANETARIUM

Children wrote letters to Tyson in protest of his position on the declassification of Pluto.

# The enthusiast!

# Chronology

## IV<sup>th</sup> CENTURY B.C.

**Euclid** studies **Thales** and writes the laws of geometry. **Aristotle** describes the world and influences centuries of Eastern and Western thought.

## X<sup>th</sup> CENTURY

**Alhazen** establishes the basics of the experimental method and opposes the influence of authoritarianism on scientific discourse.

## XVIII<sup>th</sup> CENTURY

**Lavoisier** modernizes the study of chemistry with his law of conservation of mass.

## XIX<sup>th</sup> CENTURY

**Darwin** demonstrates how the species evolved. **Mendel** develops the laws of inheritance. **Faraday** and **Maxwell** discover electromagnetism. **Mendeleev** orders the chemical elements.

## 1915

**Wegener** explains continental drift.

## 1916

**Einstein** starts to work on general relativity.

## XVI<sup>th</sup> CENTURY

**Copernicus** writes that the planets revolve around one another and the sun. **Galileo** and **Kepler** prove that this "heliocentric model" is true.

## XVII<sup>th</sup> CENTURY

**Newton** explains the movements of the planets using his theory of universal gravitation. **Harvey** describes the circulation of blood. **Descartes** argues that rationality is the criterion that should guide scientific thought.

## 1900

The first work in the field of quantum mechanics is done, with **Bohr** uniting together the world's great theorists.

## 1903

**Marie Curie** receives her first Nobel Prize for her work on radioactivity and her discoveries of polonium and radium.

## 1993

The software created by **Tim Berners-Lee** in 1989 becomes accessible to all. A new and abstract universe is born: the internet.

## 2003

The project created to map the human genome is complete, with 99.9% of genes sequenced.

Brimming with creative inspiration, how-to projects, and useful information to enrich your everyday life, Quarto Knows is a favorite destination for those pursuing their interests and passions. Visit our site and dig deeper with our books into your area of interest: Quarto Creates, Quarto Cooks, Quarto Homes, Quarto Lives, Quarto Drives, Quarto Explores, Quarto Gifts, or Quarto Kids.

Super Scientists © 2018 Gallimard Jeunesse, Paris
Translation © 2019 Quarto Publishing plc.

First Published in 2018 in French by Gallimard Jeunesse, France.
First Published in 2019 in English by Wide Eyed Editions an imprint of The Quarto Group.
400 First Avenue North, Suite 400, Minneapolis, MN 55401, USA.
T (612) 344-8100 F (612) 344-8692 **www.QuartoKnows.com**

ISBN 978-1-78603-474-8

The illustrations were created digitally
Set in Brandon Grotesque and Gotham Rounded

Translated by Lili Owen Rowlands
Edited by Lucy Brownridge
Designed by Nicola Price
Production by Nicolas Zeifman

Manufactured in Guangdong, China CC112018
9 8 7 6 5 4 3 2 1